A CATECHISM
FOR CHILDREN

A CATECHISM FOR CHILDREN

ANCHORING GOD'S WORD IN YOUR CHILD'S HEAR

BRIAN DEMBOWCZYK

A Catechism for Children
Copyright © 2014 by Brian Dembowczyk

This title is also available in a Kindle version.
Visit www.amazon.com.

To Joshua, Hannah, and Caleb.
I pray that you each fully glorify God in whatever you do.
You are each a blessing and a gift from God.

Soli Deo Gloria!

CONTENTS

WHAT IS A CATECHISM?

A catechism is a question and answer method for teaching important biblical doctrines to children. Parents ask a series of questions and help children learn and understand the answer to each. Catechisms have been used since New Testament times to help ground children, and even adults, in biblical Christian faith.

WHY USE A CATECHISM?

Your child is one of the greatest gifts God has given you (Psalm 127:3-5). As with every other gift, you are expected to be a faithful steward (Matthew 25:14-20) and take care of your child to the best of your abilities. This includes loving your child, nurturing your child, and providing your child with the basic necessities of life. While all of this is quite important, there is a provision of even greater importance: helping your child develop faith in Christ.

God's intention has always been for you, the parent, to be your child's primary Bible teacher. Unfortunately, many parents have chosen to abdicate this responsibility to the church with disastrous results. High school graduates who faithfully attended church as children and teens are leaving the church In droves. Many of the teenagers who are in churches lack the solid biblical foundation to help them make the right decisions about drugs, alcohol, sex, what they prioritize, and relationships. Clearly handing off children to a church for their spiritual development Is not working!

When you think about it, it's not surprising. Churches only have about three to four hours a week to impact a child or teen. That's about 150 to 200 hours a year; the equivalent of about one week. Now think about how much time you, the parent, have. Can you see the wisdom of God's plan for you to be your child's primary discipler? Churches surely have a role to play in this process, but it is a supporting one, not a starring one.

Deuteronomy 6:4-9 is one of the clearest passages explaining how you are to teach your own child about God. Moses offers the following instructions to Israel:

> [4] "Listen, Israel: The LORD our God, the LORD is One. [5] Love the LORD your God with all your heart, with all your soul, and with all your strength. [6] These words that I am giving you today are to be in your heart. [7] Repeat them to your children. Talk about them when you sit in your house and when you walk along the road, when you lie down and when you get up. [8] Bind them as a sign on your hand and let them be a symbol on your forehead. [9] Write them on the doorposts of your house and on your gates."

Notice that Moses does not instruct parents to hand off their children to church "experts" who will teach them about God. He calls on parents to teach their own children about God as a part of everyday life.

You have been given the same mission today. As a parent, your goal should be to saturate your family and home with biblically sound, gospel-centered conversations about God.

This is where using a catechism fits into the equation. When you look more closely at Deuteronomy 6:4-9 you can see three ways a catechism will help you:

(1) Notice in verse 7 that parents are supposed to repeat God's Word to their children. Once is not enough. It requires repetition. You know this from teaching your child in other areas of life. How many times did you need to show your child how to tie his shoes? How often did you have to encourage your daughter to use the "big girl potty?" Repetition is even more critical when it comes to biblical instruction. The idea is for you to read and recite God's Word repeatedly so that your child will memorize it. A catechism is simply a structured way to help you do this.

(2) We learn in verses 7-9 that parents are supposed to keep God's Word in front of their children at all times. As you see in the passage, this involves formal repetition of Scripture and informal conversations about God. Basically, you are to intentionally weave God into everyday life. This is strategically important. You don't want your child to perceive that God is an addition (even an important one) to everyday life. You want your child to view God as organically intertwined into the very fabric of life so much so that she cannot even conceive of life without Him. A catechism will help you position God in your home this way. Answering the catechism's questions will quickly become part of the normal flow of life. Additionally, you will find ample opportunities to follow-up the catechism instruction with spiritual conversations that help your child move past learning the *what* of the faith toward grasping the *why* of the faith.

(3) Don't miss the goal of spiritual instruction in verse 6. As a parent, you are supposed to know God's Word, but that's not where you stop. You are supposed to have God's Word in your heart. When we know biblical truth – when we really know it – a deep love for God should form within us. The same holds true for children. It is not enough to aim at placing biblical truth in your child's mind; your goal should be to anchor it within her heart so that she may deeply love God as well. While the goal is the heart, you cannot bypass the mind. Using a catechism can be a critically important first step in this process.

HOW TO USE THIS CATECHISM

If you already engage in regular discipleship activities with your child, you can use this catechism simply to supplement what you are doing. If, however, this is all new to you, right now you are either quite excited about building into your child spiritually, or you are quite intimidated. Perhaps you might even be a little of both. Know that if you are nervous and unsure, you are not alone! At the same time, be encouraged. You are almost over the first, and perhaps largest, hurdle – accepting this assignment from God. Once you choose to embrace this assignment, you can begin to put the pieces in place to fulfill it. This catechism is designed to be one of those pieces and to help you begin having regular times of spiritual development with your child.

When to Start

You'd be surprised at how much preschoolers, and even toddlers, can learn. If your child is a preschooler or toddler, it's not too early to start using this catechism. While you might need to eliminate or decrease the expectation of your child being able to answer the questions on his or her own, you can still read the questions and answers to your child to begin the repetition process. Parents of infants may even want to begin reading the weekly catechism question to their baby to develop the habit early. If your child is in Kindergarten or grade school, he should be able to interact with you by answering the questions.

How to Start

The catechism is designed to feature one question per week. Begin by picking a day and time that is easiest for you to protect on a regular basis. Ideally this would be at the start of the week, but it is more important that you select a day you can guard. You shouldn't need long; fifteen minutes would be plenty of time. Don't worry about beginning at the start of a calendar year or month. You can jump into teaching this catechism at any point.

This catechism is divided into three 48 question units. Each unit is designed to last one year. *Unit 1* focuses on God and the Bible. *Unit 2* focuses on Man & Sin, Salvation, and Evangelism & Missions. *Unit 3* focuses on the Church, Christian Living, the Family, and Last Things. If you are partnering with a church or group of parents, you will want to start where they are. If you are doing this on your own, it is best to start with *Unit 1* and work straight through the catechism from the beginning. The reason 52 questions are not provided per unit will be explained below.

What to Do

During your weekly time, introduce that week's new catechism question. Repeat the question during the week to help your child learn it. You might want to ask the current week's question at meal times, at bedtime, on the way to school, or simply randomly as the day unfolds. The important thing to remember is that you continue to ask the question repeatedly and look for follow-up conversations related to it.

A Suggested Family Devotion Plan

If you do not already have a plan for weekly family devotions, here's a suggested model for you to use:

1) *Review previous catechism questions.* Ask your child the last few catechism questions and perhaps review all the questions from the current topic or unit.

2) *Introduce the new catechism question.* Read the new question but don't provide the answer. Give your child a chance to answer. If she cannot, then share the answer.

3) *Read the supporting Bible passages together.* Nearly every question includes supporting Bible passages. No question has more than four; most have three. This was done to make it possible for you to read each passage during the devotion time. You will notice that some of the supporting passages have an asterisk (*) by them. These are suggested memory verses.

4) *Talk about the catechism question and passages.* Give your child an opportunity to ask questions he may

have. You may also want to ask your child follow-up questions, offer explanations, and personalize what you are discussing. For example, when talking about God being everywhere (*Unit 1*, Question 4) you may want to teach an older child the term "omnipresent." You may also want to provide an illustration of this challenging concept for a younger child such as, "While we cannot see God, we know He is everywhere. Just like we cannot see the air, but we know it is there."

5) *Practice the month's memory verse.* Twelve suggested memory verses are included with each unit. These verses relate to the topics being studied and can be used to help your child to begin, or continue, memorizing Scripture. Of course if your child is older and adept at memorizing Bible passages, you may want to increase the amount of verses or select more challenging ones. If your child is younger, you may need to reduce the number and/or simplify the verses.

6) *Pray.* Give your child a chance to pray as you wrap up your time together. Encourage your child to pray about the truth you learned from this week's catechism question (for example, "Thank you for always being there when I need you.") as well as anything else on her heart. Even if your child prays, you will want to pray as well. Praying for your child and with her is one of the greatest activities in which you can engage. Here are a few elements you might want to include regularly in your prayer:

- Thank God for giving you your child

- Ask God to protect your child
- Ask God to help your child learn about Him and love Him
- Pray that your child is an example of God's love to her friends
- Pray that God helps you to be the father or mother your child deserves

Missional Living Opportunities

You may be wondering why the catechism features 48 questions per year instead of 52. This gives you a chance to conduct a special quarterly family devotion time. Whenever you have a fifth devotion night within a month put your faith in God to practice.

Arrange for your family to volunteer at a homeless shelter, food pantry, clothing closet, or some other ministry. Show God's love to a neighbor by raking their leaves, cleaning a flower bed, painting a porch, or washing their car. Take a meal to a shut-in, some home-made get-well cards to someone in the hospital, or a small token of appreciation to a pastor, Bible study teacher, or school teacher.

You also might want to establish a tradition of spending some quality family time together as part of this quarterly event. Stop for ice cream afterward. Go to an arcade. Play games together. The chances are good that it won't take long for your family to cherish these quarterly special events.

Some Final Tips

Here are a few final suggestions and reminders as you get started:

1) *Consistency is key.* Do your best to guard your catechism/family devotion time.

2) *Don't worry about word-for-word memorization.* It is more important that your child learns the concepts.

3) *Don't just focus on the facts.* Learning the catechism is not the goal; it is simply a tool to help you achieve your goal of anchoring God in your child's heart.

4) *Struggle with your child.* As your child struggles to understand God show him that you don't have it all figured out either. Don't be ashamed of the greatness of God and our limitations to comprehend Him.

5) *Grow with your child.* Don't be surprised if you learn a few things as you work through this catechism with your child.

6) *Enjoy the journey.* Teaching your child about God is indeed a great responsibility, but it is also an amazing blessing. It is exciting to see God work in your child and to know that you are making an impact on her spiritual development.

UNIT 1

God

Question1

Q. How many gods are there?

A. There is only one true God.

Deuteronomy 6:4*; Psalm 96:4-5; 1 Timothy 1:17

Note: Many other religions believe in many gods. Hindus, for example, believe in tens of thousands of gods. The Bible presents only one true God.

Question 2

Q. In how many persons does God exist?

A. He is one God in three persons.

Matthew 28:19*; 2 Corinthians 13:14; 1 Peter 1:2

Note: This is a very difficult concept to understand. You may want to talk about how we cannot know everything about God because He is infinite and we are finite. Let your child know it is ok to have unanswered questions about God. A way to illustrate this might be a computer. Most of us can't even begin to understand how computers work, but we are content not knowing. Not understanding how the computer works does not detract from our enjoyment of using it. The same is true of God. Just because we might not understand certain aspects of God doesn't mean we cannot enjoy knowing Him.

Question 3

Q. Who are the three persons of God?

A. God the Father, God the Son, and God the Holy Spirit.
Matthew 28:19*; 2 Corinthians 13:14; 1 Peter 1:2

Note: While the term "Trinity" does not appear in the Bible, the concept is quite clear. Some people prefer to use the term "Triunity" instead to emphasize the unity of God (Question 1).

Question 4

Q. Where is God?

A. Everywhere.
Psalm 139:7-12; Jeremiah 23:23-24

Note: You may want to introduce the term "omnipresent" which means God is everywhere.

Question 5

Q. Is there anything or anyone greater than God?

A. No, He is greater and better than everything.
1 Samuel 2:2; Psalm 96:4; Isaiah 44:6

Note: While many things in life are quite enjoyable and satisfying, ultimately God has designed us to find true contentment and joy only in knowing Him.

Question 6
Q. How much authority does God have?
A. He has all authority.
Psalm 135:6; Daniel 4:35; Ephesians 1:11

Note: You may want to introduce the term "sovereign" which means God has absolute authority as a King, Lord, or Master.

Question 7
Q. Does God know all things?
A. Yes, He knows everything that is, everything that was, everything that will be, and everything that could be.
1 Chronicles 28:9; Psalm 147:5; Luke 12:6-7

Note: You may want to introduce the term "omniscient" which means all-knowing.

Question 8
Q. Can God do all things?
A. Yes, He can do anything according to His character.
Deuteronomy 3:24; Jeremiah 32:17; Daniel 4:34-5

Note: You may want to introduce the term "omnipotent" which means all-powerful. While God can do all things, there are actually limits He has placed on Himself because of His character. For example, God cannot sin because, by nature, He is holy. He cannot lie either because He is true. God's omnipotence is thus "limited" by His nature.

Question 9
Q. Is God perfect?
A. Yes, He is perfect and holy in all of His characteristics.
Leviticus 11:44; Isaiah 6:3; Revelation 4:8

Note: Some theologians refer to God's characteristics as His "attributes" while others call them His "perfections." God is perfect in each one of His characteristics and cannot improve or regress in any one of them.

Question 10
Q. Was God created?
A. No, He has always existed.
Exodus 3:14; Psalm 90:2; 1 Timothy 1:17

Note: When we say that God has always existed, or that He is eternal, we actually mean that He is outside of time. Time was created by God when He created the universe. This is another hard concept for us to grasp because we are anchored in time and struggle to even imagine timelessness.

Question 11
Q. Does God the Father have a body?
A. No, He is spirit.
Numbers 23:19; John 4:24*

Note: God has no physical aspect, in part because the physical realm was created by Him. Furthermore, He is infinite and therefore cannot be reduced and limited within a physical body.

Question 12
Q. By what name do we know God the Son?
A. Jesus.
Matthew 1:1; 1:21; Mark 1:1

Note: Jesus is derived from the Hebrew name, Joshua, which means "God delivers." It is a fitting name for Jesus' earthly ministry.

Question 13
Q. What else do we call Jesus?
A. The Christ, or the Messiah.
Matthew 1:1; 1:16; Acts 2:36

Note: "Christ" and "Messiah" mean the same thing, "the anointed one." Christ is based on the Greek language of the New Testament, while Messiah is based on the Hebrew language of the Old Testament.

Question 14
Q. Why did Jesus become a man?
A. To please His Father and provide forgiveness for sin.
Romans 8:3; Philippians 2:5-8; Hebrews 2:14, 17

Note: While the Son of God is eternal, He did have a "beginning" as a man when He was born to Mary.

Question 15

Q. How was Jesus born?

A. By the virgin, Mary.

Luke 1:31,35; John 1:14

Note: The Bible teaches that the Holy Spirit brought this process about. The virgin birth was necessary because sin is inherited; therefore because Jesus was not born like all other men, He was shielded from having a sin nature.

Question 16

Q. Is Jesus God or man?

A. He is both fully God and fully man.

John 1:1; Philippians 2:5-8; Colossians 2:9

Note: Jesus is fully God and fully man without compromise or mixture of either characteristic. Being a man makes Him no less God; being God makes Him no less a man.

Question 17

Q. Did Jesus ever sin?

A. No, He was sinless and blameless.

Hebrews 4:15; 7:26; 1 John 3:5

Note: The Bible records that Jesus was tempted, but did not give-in to that temptation. This is important for two reasons. First, we know Jesus understands our struggle with sin because He can with us. Second, because He was sinless, His sacrifice on the cross was perfect and acceptable to God.

Question 18

Q. What did Jesus do to provide forgiveness?

A. He died on the cross for those who believe.

Isaiah 53:4-6; Romans 5:8-11*; Ephesians 1:7

Note: God promised all the way back in Eden that death would be required for sin. The beauty of the gospel is that God provided a substitute to pay that death penalty in Jesus.

Question 19

Q. Did Jesus actually die?

A. Yes, and then buried for three days and three nights.

Mark 15:43-45; John 19:32-34; 1 Corinthians 15:3*

Note: Some critics argue that there was no resurrection because Jesus never died in the first place. The argument suggests that Jesus passed out on the cross and was revived in the tomb. There are two major problems with this claim. First, the Roman guards were experts in killing prisoners and verified that Jesus was dead. Second, how could Jesus have unwrapped Himself from the burial wrappings, removed the stone blocking the grave, and escaped the guards especially after having been whipped, beaten, and crucified?

Question 20

Q. What happened to Jesus on the third day?

A. He rose from the dead and left the grave.
Luke 24:45-7; John 20:1-8; 1 Corinthians 15:4*

Note: The math doesn't seem to support that Jesus was in the grave for "three days and three nights." Jesus died on a Friday afternoon and raised on Sunday morning which consists of three days (Friday, Saturday, and Sunday) and two nights (Friday, and Saturday). However, in first century Israel, any part of a day was phrased "a day and a night." By this definition, Jesus was in the grave for "three days and three nights."

Question 21

Q. Can we prove that Jesus rose from the dead?

A. Yes, there were many witnesses.
1 Corinthians 15:5-8

Note: There is sufficient historical and archaeological evidence to support the life, death, and resurrection of Jesus. The question of the empty tomb stands to this day. How can it be explained apart from the resurrection? Dozens of people saw Jesus. No one ever produced His body. His followers lived radically different lives and many even gave their lives for their faith.

Question 22

Q. Did Jesus have a body after raising from the dead?

A. Yes, it was like His body before, but it was also different.

Luke 24:36-43

Note: After the resurrection, Jesus was recognized by His followers, so His appearance was similar. He maintained the wounds in His hands, feet, and side. He ate food. However, He passed through a wall and seemed to travel a great distance instantly. It is believed that our future resurrected bodies will likewise be similar in ways and yet different in other ways.

Question 23

Q. Is the Holy Spirit a person?

A. Yes, He is a person just like the Father and the Son.

1 Corinthians 2:10; 12:11; Ephesians 4:30

Note: Many people have no problem recognizing Jesus and God the Father as persons, but struggle to see the Holy Spirit as a person. For example many Christians refer to the Holy Spirit as "It" instead of "Him." Personhood is comprised of three key factors: intellect, will, and emotion. The Holy Spirit demonstrates all three of these.

Question 24
Q. Where is the Holy Spirit?
A. Living in believers.
John 14:16; Romans 5:5; 1 Corinthians 2:12

Note: One of the primary ministries of the Holy Spirit is to "seal" the believer for salvation. Think of how kings sent letters a long time ago. The king would write a letter on paper and then roll the paper. Hot wax would be used to seal the letter closed and then the king would impress his signet ring into the hot wax symbolizing the letter was his property and that it was not to be trifled with. The Holy Spirit serves the same purpose identifying believers as being owned by God.

Question 25
Q. Does everyone have the Holy Spirit?
A. No, only those who believe in Jesus.
Romans 8:9; 1 Corinthians 2:14; Jude 19

Note: While the Holy Spirit convicts unbelievers of their sin in the process of leading them to salvation, He does not indwell them like He does believers.

Question 26
Q. How does the Holy Spirit help us to read the Bible?
A. He shows us what is true.
John 14:26; 16:13; 1 Corinthians 2:11

Note: While there are many great tools available to help us read the Bible, our greatest help comes from the Holy Spirit who guides all believers toward truth.

Question 27
Q. How does the Holy Spirit help us to repent?
A. He shows us when we sin.
John 16:8-11; Acts 2:37

Note: "Repent" will be defined in *Unit 2*, Question 23. You may want to define it here as well. While everyone has a conscience that guides behavior, that is not the same as the Holy Spirit convicting a person of sin. Conscience is most often based on societal norms and a desire to avoid negative consequences of actions. The Holy Spirit convicts based on the perfect standard of God.

Question 28
Q. How does the Holy Spirit help us to be forgiven?
A. He gives us new life.
John 3:5; Titus 3:5

Note: You may want to introduce the term, "regeneration" which means being given new life. When a person experiences God's forgiveness through Christ for the first time, he becomes a new person. While he may look the same, and might even act similarly at first, the truth is that he is a new person and he will begin to live differently.

Question 29

Q. How does the Holy Spirit help us when life is difficult?

A. He comforts us and gives us peace.

John 14:16; Romans 8:26

Note: At times, the Holy Spirit is called the "Comforter" in the Bible. He comes alongside believers and provides emotional, mental, and spiritual comfort in times of difficulty.

Question 30

Q. How does the Holy Spirit help us to obey God?

A. He gives us power to live for God.

Acts 1:8; Galatians 5:16; 5:22-23*

Note: All believers are called on by God to obey Him. The wonderful thing is that God also gives us the power and ability to obey Him. When we try to obey God in our own power, we will end up frustrated and disappointed because we are not meant to accomplish this through our own abilities or will. When we allow God to work in us, we will experience success and joy.

Question 31

Q. What gifts does the Holy Spirit give?

A. He gives spiritual gifts to help us serve God.
Romans 12:6-8; 1 Corinthians 12:1-31; Ephesians 4:7-16; 1 Peter 4:10-11

Note: Every believer has been given at least one spiritual gift to be used. If you are unsure about what gift you might have, you can complete a spiritual gift inventory or ask someone who knows you well what she has observed in your life.

The Bible

Question 32

Q. What is the Bible?

A. God's revelation (explanation) of Himself to us.
John 20:31; 2 Timothy 3:16-17; 2 Peter 1:21*

Note: While we can see the "fingerprints" of God in His creation, the only way we can truly know of Him is through the Bible. All that we know of God is that which He has chosen to reveal to us. There is much more to God that He has chosen not to reveal.

Question 33

Q. Who wrote the Bible?

A. Men who were inspired by the Holy Spirit.
2 Timothy 3:16; 1 Peter 1:10-11; 2 Peter 1:20-21*

Note: You may want to introduce the term, "inspiration" which concerns how the writers of the Bible were moved by God to write perfectly the Bible. Inspiration allowed the writers to write in their own style, but covers the very words of Scripture.

Question 34

Q. How many parts are in the Bible?

A. Two parts; the Old and New Testaments.

Note: The terms "Old Covenant" and "New Covenant" could be used as well. These terms highlight the nature of the Old Testament focusing on living under the Mosaic Law and the New Testament focusing on living under grace in Christ.

Question 35

Q. How many books are in the Bible?

A. 66; 39 in the Old Testament and 27 in the New Testament.

Note: Some of the tests used to determine which books belonged in the Bible included who the author was (a prophet, someone who knew Jesus, etc.), if the book was widely accepted by the early church; any claim of the book to be divine (such as including the term, "thus says the Lord"), and the absence of error – theological, historical, or otherwise.

Question 36

Q. What are the five divisions of the Old Testament?

A. The law, history, writings, major prophets, and minor prophets.

Note: The differentiation between the major and minor prophets concerns length of the books, not importance.

Question 37

Q. What are the five divisions of the New Testament?

A. The Gospels, history, Pauline epistles, general epistles, and prophecy.

Note: "Epistle" means letter.

Question 38

Q. What is the ultimate purpose of the Bible?

A. To guide people to salvation in Jesus.
Luke 24:27, 44; 2 Timothy 3:14-15

Note: The Bible is one comprehensive and cohesive story of how God went about redeeming fallen man to Himself through Jesus Christ. The basic narrative can be viewed this way: Genesis 1-2 describes God's perfect creation. Genesis 3 through Revelation 20 describes man's fall and struggle under the curse as well as God's provision of Jesus. Revelation 21-22 describes the universe restored and made right again as in Eden.

Question 39

Q. What else does the Bible teach us?

A. How we should live.

Psalm 19:7-11; 119:104; 2 Timothy 3:16-17*

Note: While the Bible should not be read as a collection of moral stories that help us to live better (it is all about Jesus; see question 38), it does share with us how we should live in a way that reflects the character of Jesus and pleases God.

Question 40

Q. Is there any untruth in the Bible?

A. No, it is all true and has no error.

Psalm 19:9; John 17:17; 2 Timothy 3:16*

Note: You may want to introduce the term, "inerrancy" which means without error.

Question 41

Q. What do the first four of the Ten Commandments concern?

A. Our relationship with God.

Exodus 20:1-11; Deuteronomy 5:1-15

Note: Often called the first "table" of the Ten Commandments, these four concern our vertical relationship with God.

Question 42

Q. What does the Fifth Commandment concern?

A. Our relationship with our parents.

Exodus 20:12; Deuteronomy 5:16

Note: This commandment is considered a "hinge" because it can concern our relationship with God (our Heavenly Father) or our earthly fathers.

Question 43

Q. What do the last five of the Ten Commandments concern?

A. Our relationship with others.

Exodus 20:13-17; Deuteronomy 5:17-22

Note: The second "table" of the Ten Commandments concerns our horizontal relationships with others.

Question 44

Q. What do the Ten Commandments teach us?

A. To love God and love people.

Matthew 22:37-40*; Mark 12:28-33

Note: The two tables of the Ten Commandments reveal that it is impossible to love God and not love others. Likewise, we cannot truly love others if we do not have the love of God in us. These two aspects of life are intertwined and cannot be separated – just like the Ten Commandments picture.

Question 45

Q. Can any person obey all Ten Commandments?

A. No, it is impossible.

Ecclesiastes 7:20; Romans 3:23*; James 2:10; 1 John 1:8

Note: On the surface it seems like we might be able to obey at least a few of the Commandments, such as not murdering. However, there are two problems with this. First, the Bible says that if we violate one law, even a "minor" one, we have violated the entire Law. Second, Jesus raised the standard of the Ten Commandments in the Sermon on the Mount focusing attention on the condition of our hearts. For example, instead of using physical murder as the standard of measurement, Jesus called on us to use hate, something of which we are all guilty.

Question 46

Q. What then is the purpose of the Ten Commandments and Old Testament Law?

A. To show us our sinfulness and need for grace.

Romans 3:20; 7:7; Galatians 3:22,24

Note: The Ten Commandments and entire set of 613 Old Testament laws exist to show us how futile it is to try to earn God's favor by our conduct. We can never be good enough (perfection), and therefore we are all trapped in a terrible problem because of our sin. In short, we need another way out of our sin problem.

Question 47
Q. What is the greatest commandment?
A. To love God.
Matthew 22:37-38*

Note: When a lawyer (someone who was well-versed in the Old Testament law) asked Jesus which of the 613 commands He thought was most important, Jesus referred to Deuteronomy 6:5 which shares our need to love God fully. Only from genuine love for God comes worthy obedience.

Question 48
Q. What is the second greatest commandment?
A. To love others.
Matthew 22:39*

Note: Although the lawyer asked only for the (singular) greatest commandment, Jesus offered the second greatest commandment as well. This time Jesus pointed to Leviticus 19:18 which emphasizes our need to love others. Jesus then claimed the entire law is based on these two primary commandments. Just like in the Ten Commandments, we see that loving God and loving people are tied together.

SUGGESTED MEMORY VERSES

January
In the beginning God created the heavens and the earth. **Genesis 1:1**

February
"Listen, Israel: The LORD our God, the LORD is One." **Deuteronomy 6:4**

March
This book of instruction must not depart from your mouth; you are to recite it day and night, so that you may carefully observe everything written in it. For then you will prosper and succeed in whatever you do. **Joshua 1:8**

April
God is our refuge and strength, a helper who is always found in times of trouble. **Psalm 46:1**

May
He has told you men what is good and what it is the LORD requires of you: Only to act justly, to love faithfulness, and to walk humbly with your God. **Micah 6:8**

June
He said to him, "Love the Lord your God with all your heart, with all your soul, and with all your mind. This is the greatest and most important commandment. The second is like it: Love your neighbor as yourself. All the Law and the Prophets depend on these two commandments." **Matthew 22:37-40**

July

Then Jesus came near and said to them, "All authority has been given to Me in heaven and on earth. Go, therefore, and make disciples of all nations, baptizing them in the name of the Father and of the Son and of the Holy Spirit, teaching them to observe everything I have commanded you. And remember, I am with you always, to the end of the age." **Matthew 28:18-20**

August

"God is spirit, and those who worship Him must worship in spirit and truth." **John 4:24**

September

"Peace I leave with you. My peace I give to you. I do not give to you as the world gives. Your heart must not be troubled or fearful." **John 14:27**

October

Therefore, whether you eat or drink, or whatever you do, do everything for God's glory. **1 Corinthians 10:31**

November

But the fruit of the Spirit is love, joy, peace, patience, kindness, goodness, faith, gentleness, self-control. Against such things there is no law. **Galatians 5:22-23**

December

All Scripture is inspired by God and is profitable for teaching, for rebuking, for correcting, for training in righteousness, so that the man of God may be complete, equipped for every good work. **2 Timothy 3:16-17**

UNIT 2

Man and Sin

Question 1
Q. Who were the first people God created?
A. Adam and Eve.
Genesis 2:7,18-25; Acts 17:26; 1 Timothy 2:13

Note: Adam means "man" and is from the Hebrew word for "ground." Eve means "life" or "life-producer."

Question 2
Q. How did God create Adam?
A. From dirt.
Genesis 2:7; 3:19; Psalm 103:14

Note: Adam's body was formed out of the ground, but his life came from the breath of God. In this way mankind is distinct from animals which did not receive the breath of God and are not created in His image.

Question 3
Q. How did God create Eve?
A. From a rib out of Adam.
Genesis 2:21-23

Note: God most likely chose to create Eve in this manner so that Adam and Eve would have an immediate and deep bond right away.

Question 4
Q. What did God give Adam and Eve besides a body?
A. A soul.
Ecclesiastes 12:7; Zechariah 12:1; 1 Corinthians 15:45

Note: A person's soul is the true essence of his or her identity.

Question 5
Q. In what condition did God make Adam and Eve?
A. Perfect, innocent, and content.
Genesis 1:26-31; Psalm 8:4-8; Ecclesiastes 7:29

Note: When created, Adam and Eve were completely perfect. This does not mean they were infinite like God, but it does mean they conformed to God's perfect standard.

Question 6
Q. Did Adam and Eve stay perfect, innocent, and content?
A. No, they sinned against God.
Genesis 3:1-7; Ecclesiastes 7:29; Romans 5:12

Note: As soon as Adam and Eve rebelled against God, they stopped being perfect, innocent, and content. Sin completely ruined what God had created.

Question 7

Q. What is sin?

A. Not being who God created me to be by either doing what He forbids or not doing what He commands.
1 Samuel 15:22-3; Matthew 5:48; Romans 1:21-32

Note: Some people refer to sins of "commission" (doing what is wrong) and "omission" (not doing what is right). It is important to understand that sin also concerns our attitude, not just what we do.

Question 8

Q. How did Adam and Eve sin against God?

A. They rebelled against God by eating the forbidden fruit.
Genesis 2:16-7; 3:6

Note: When Adam and Eve ate the fruit, that was an external action of an inward choice to disbelieve God and rebel against Him. Eating the fruit proved their rejection of God's plan for their lives.

Question 9

Q. Who tempted Adam and Eve to sin?

A. The devil tempted Eve and she gave the fruit to Adam who was with her.
Genesis 3:1-13; 2 Corinthians 11:3; 1 Timothy 2:13-4

Note: The Bible does not indicate that the fruit was an apple. Some believe it may have been a pomegranate while others think it may have been a fig.

Question 10

Q. Who is responsible for Adam and Eve sinning?

A. Adam and Eve are responsible because they freely chose to disobey God.
Genesis 3:8-19; Acts 2:23; James 1:13-15

Note: While Satan played a role, Adam and Eve were still accountable for their sin. Others may influence us to sin and even make it easy to sin, but ultimately we have no one to blame but ourselves when we sin against God.

Question 11

Q. What happened to Adam and Eve when they ate the forbidden fruit?

A. They became sinful and separated from God.
Genesis 3:14-24; 4:1-24; James 1:14-5

Note: True to God's word, Adam and Eve would eventually die. This promise of death because of disobedience is reinforced by the account of Cain killing Abel (4:1-14), Lamech bragging about killing a man and a boy (4:23-24), and the first genealogy in chapter 5 mentioning "and he died" over and over.

Question 12

Q. What effect did Adam and Eve's sin have on all people?

A. Everyone is born with a sin nature.
Psalm 51:5; Romans 5:12; 1 Corinthians 15:21-2

Note: Because Adam and Eve sinned, all people who have

been born to them are born in sin. Unlike what many people want to believe, people are not born innocent – we are all born in sin.

Question 13
Q. What does every sin deserve?
A. Death and separation from a holy God.
Romans 6:23*; Galatians 3:10; Ephesians 5:6

Note: While the consequences of sin vary, making some more severe than others, the judgment is the same. If the only sin a person ever committed was telling a "little white lie," that would still condemn them the same as murder. The reason is because God is perfect and cannot accept any imperfection, no matter how seemingly small to us.

Question 14
Q. Can people have a relationship with God and be sinful?
A. No, because God is perfect.
Joshua 24:19; Isaiah 6:5; Hebrews 9:3-10

Note: An illustration might be helpful. Imagine a glass of pure drinking water. How much poison would you add before a.) it is no longer pure and b.) you refrain from drinking? God cannot accept any amount of sin, no matter how seemingly small, and retain His perfection.

Question 15
Q. Who made you?
A. God

Genesis 1:26-7; Psalm 139:13; Acts 17:24-29

Note: God is the Creator of all things including each individual person. This should be the foundation of each person's value and self-worth.

Question 16
Q. Did God give you a soul as well?
A. Yes.

Ecclesiastes 12:7; Zechariah 12:1; Mark 12:30

Note: Your soul is the essence of who you truly are. While we tend to identify people based on their appearance or by what name they are called, those aspects of a person may change.

Question 17
Q. What else did God make?
A. Everything.

Genesis 1*; Acts 14:15; Colossians 1:16

Note: Everything is made by God and consequently belongs to God.

Question 18
Q. Why did God make all things?
A. For His own glory.
Psalm 19:1; 1 Corinthians 10:31*; Revelation 4:11

Note: God's glory concerns His magnificence, splendor, and fame. Everything exists to reveal how amazing God is.

Question 19
Q. How can you glorify God?
A. By loving Him and obeying Him.
Mark 12:29-31; John 15:8-10; 1 Corinthians 10:31

Note: The simplest way to communicate how a person can glorify God is to say she should love God (the Greatest Commandment) and out of that love obey God. It is vital that loving God is positioned as the most important aspect of glorifying God. Obedience without love leads to legalism and religion instead of grace-based relationship.

Question 20
Q. Why should you glorify God?
A. Because He made me and takes care of me.
Romans 11:36; Revelation 4:11

Note: The simplest way to communicate the reason for glorifying God is to affirm God as our Creator, owner, and provider.

Salvation

Question 21

Q. Do people have to die and stay separated from God?
A. No, there is a way to be forgiven and saved.
Isaiah 53:11; Romans 3:19-20, 23; 8:29-30

Note: Some people are unhappy with the gospel because it requires us to recognize that God is holy and just and holds people accountable for sin. People often ask, "Why would a loving God send people to hell?" There are two problems with this question. First, God sends no one to hell – people choose to go there because of their rebellion. Second, God has provided the means for anyone who accepts the gospel to be saved. The gospel is truly "good news."

Question 22

Q. Who will be saved?
A. Those who repent of sin and have faith in Jesus.
Mark 1:15; Luke 13:3,5; Acts 2:37-41; Romans 10:13*

Note: The gospel is not limited to people of a certain gender, race, economic position, age, or culture. It is applicable to anyone, anywhere, at any time. We are all equal in our need for forgiveness and we all have the same access to be saved if we repent and believe in Jesus.

Question 23

Q. What does it mean to repent?

A. To turn away from sin and turn toward God.

Romans 6:1-2; 2 Corinthians 7:9-11; 1 Thessalonians 1:9-10

Note: Biblical repentance can be thought of as "turning." It involves an act of the will to change your mind and actions. One must turn from sin and rebellion and turn to God. Simply turning from sin is not enough. Repentance also requires the person to turn to God and choose to live His way.

Question 24

Q. What does it mean to have faith in Jesus?

A. Knowing who Jesus is, accepting His payment for your sin, and wanting to follow Him in life.

John 1:12; Romans 10:9; 1 John 5:11-12

Note: The Bible uses "faith," "trust," "belief," and even "obedience" to describe what a person must possess to be saved. It is more than an intellectual assent, it also involves trusting one's life to God.

A Catechism for Children

Question 25

Q. What is another word for Jesus paying our punishment in our place?

A. The atonement.

Romans 3:24-26; 2 Corinthians 5:19-21; 1 Peter 3:18

Note: "Atonement" means payment. This concept is also called the "substitionary atonement" which emphasizes that Jesus was the person's substitute in paying his or her sin penalty.

Question 26

Q. Is there another way to be saved other than Jesus?

A. No, He alone is the way to be saved.

John 14:6*; Acts 4:12; 1 Timothy 2:5

Note: Some people want to believe that all religions lead to the same destination and that people simply call God by different names. The problem with this inclusive thinking is that the Bible leaves absolutely no room for this inclusiveness. The Bible declares that only Jesus leads to salvation. So if the Bible is correct then all other religions must be wrong.

Question 27

Q. How were people saved before Jesus came to earth?

A. By faith that God would provide Jesus one day.

1 Corinthians 10:1-4; Galatians 3:8-9; Hebrews 11:13

Note: If Jesus is the only way to be saved, how were Moses, David, Isaiah and so forth be saved before Jesus came? The answer is that salvation has always been by faith. Before Jesus came, people were required to place their faith in the promise of God to send a Deliverer for them. So David's salvation was based on his trust that God would send Jesus in the future. They may have not known all of the details, but they were accountable to believe in what God had revealed to that point.

Question 28

Q. How did people in the Old Testament show their faith?

A. By offering animal sacrifices to God.

Exodus 24:3-8; Hebrews 9:19-23; 10:1-4

Note: Sacrificing animals did not provide forgiveness, it merely demonstrated a person's awareness of his need for forgiveness and his faith in God that He forgives. It also served as an act of obedience.

Question 29

Q. What did these sacrifices represent?

A. Jesus, who would one day be the perfect sacrifice.

John 1:29; Hebrews 9-10; 1 Peter 1:19

Note: While animal sacrifices were symbols of a person's faith in God, they were also a vivid picture of a person being right with God only as a result of another's shedding of blood and loss of life. This a clear picture of Jesus and the cross.

Question 30

Q. What is regeneration?

A. A new spiritual birth that involves receiving a new heart that loves God.

John 3:3; Ephesians 2:5-8*; Titus 3:5

Note: The Bible says that people are dead in their sin against God. This requires a person receiving new life (being born again) when he or she comes to Christ. When a person is regenerated, he or she takes on a new character and is able to do what he or she could not do before (such as love and please God).

Question 31

Q. Who can change a sinner's heart?

A. Only the Holy Spirit.

John 3:6; Romans 8:6-11; Titus 3:5-6

Note: Because we are so stained by sin, we need the Holy Spirit to work in our hearts so that we can acknowledge our sinfulness and God's greatness, and respond to the gospel. The Holy Spirit is like the emergency room crash cart that is used to shock a heart that has stopped beating so that it will live once again.

Question 32
Q. What is justification?
A. God declaring a sinner righteous.
Zechariah 3:1-5; Romans 3:24-26; Philippians 3:9

Note: Justification involves a person's position, or standing, with God. Think of a judge in a courtroom declaring the defendant "not guilty." In that moment, the person's standing has changed from possible guilt to complete innocence. Justification is God's declaration that we are innocent in Christ.

Question 33
Q. What does it mean to be righteous?
A. To be in right standing with God and to have Jesus' goodness in us.
Exodus 33:19; Romans 5:19; 1 John 2:29

Note: Like justification, righteousness primarily describes a person's position or standing with God. Because of Jesus, a Christian is viewed by God as completely righteous. However, a person still can live righteously (living up to his position) or unrighteously (not living up to his position).

Question 34
Q. Can anyone be saved by his own righteousness?
A. No, no one is good enough.
Ecclesiastes 7:20; Romans 3:10-23; Philippians 3:8-9

Note: Many people think that they can be right with God by doing enough good works. The thought is that if their good works outweigh their bad works, they are ok. This is not what the Bible teaches. First, no amount of good works can erase even the slightest bad work (sin) against perfect God. Second, even the greatest effort to do enough good will fail because God's established standard is perfection.

Question 35
Q. What is sanctification?
A. Growing to look and live more like Jesus.
Ephesians 2:10; 4:22-24; Philippians 2:12-13

Note: Sanctification concerns a Christian's gradual growth to live more like Jesus. It comes from the same word from which we get "holy" and means to be made holy or "set apart" from the world. You may be familiar with the part of the church building that is commonly called the "sanctuary." It is called that because it is generally set apart for worship and is rarely, if ever, used for other activities.

Question 36
Q. Will we ever look and live completely like Jesus on earth?
A. No, we should get closer and closer, but it won't be completed until heaven.
Philippians 3:12-15; 2 Peter 1:4-8; 1 John 3:1-3

Note: Although it is impossible for us to be completely like Jesus on earth, that does not mean we should not seek to grow more like Him every day. Think of a professional baseball player. Just because he will never be able to hit a home run every time at bat does not mean he should not work at becoming a better player and have a goal to hit a home run every time he is at the plate. Just because we will not be perfect followers of Jesus on earth does not mean we shouldn't try to be better followers of Jesus.

Question 37
Q. What is adoption?
A. Being made a child of God's.
John 1:12; Galatians 4:7; Ephesians 1:5

Note: You might hear people say that we are all children of God. That's actually not true. While everyone is created by God, only followers of Christ are His children because they have been adopted by God as such.

Question 38
Q. What is glorification?
A. When believers and all things are made completely right and perfect again.
1 Corinthians 15:38-50; 2 Corinthians 5:1-5; Philippians 3:20-21

Note: Because of sin, the entire universe is in a fallen state and is a mere shadow of God's original intention. However, through Christ, God is redeeming all things and making all things right again.

Question 39
Q. When will we be glorified?
A. In heaven.
Revelation 21:1-5

Note: We will experience the fullness of what it means to be a follower of Christ in heaven when we are made perfect once again and will not sin ever again. In time, we will also be given glorified bodies that are free from blemishes – physical, mental, and emotional.

Question 40
Q. Can believers lose their salvation?
A. No, all true believers endure to the end.
John 10:27-29; Romans 8:29-30; 8:35-39

Note: Some people believe that it is possible for a believer to lose his salvation; however, the stronger evidence in the Bible supports believers not being able to lose, or even forfeit, their salvation. The Bible says that Jesus gives eternal life, not the potential for eternal life, that no one (including the believer himself) can snatch a believer out of God's hands, and that a Christian is a new creation. Much like a butterfly cannot become a caterpillar again, a Christian cannot become unsaved again.

Question 41

Q. Do believers continue to sin?

A. Yes, although all their sin is forgiven.
Romans 7:15-25; 1 John 1:8

Note: When a person comes to Christ and experiences saving faith, all of his sin is forgiven – past, present, and future. Accepting Christ and receiving forgiveness is a one-time event. Sin, therefore, does not impact a person's relationship with God, but may hinder his fellowship with God. Think of it this way: a son could never do anything to change the fact that he is his father's son. The relationship is secure. However, the son can do many things to strain the fellowship he has with his father.

Question 42

Q. Should Christians sin?

A. No, our love for God and gratitude to God should compel us not to.
Romans 6:15; 1 Timothy 6:11; 2 Timothy 2:22

Note: Although we must acknowledge that we continue to sin even after coming to Christ, that does not mean it is acceptable to continue to sin without care. Some people mistakenly abuse grace and believe that if God has forgiven them completely they can live however they want. This is the opposite of what it means to live under grace. When a person experiences God's grace, she should be so overwhelmed by love and gratitude that she should desire to please God and resist sin.

55

Question 43

Q. How can Christians resist sinning?

A. Through the power of the Holy Spirit.

Galatians 3:3; Ephesians 5:18

Note: Wanting to abstain from sinning and actually abstaining are two different issues. Wanting to stop sinning comes from a heart that has been changed by God. Actually resisting sin comes from the power of God at work in the believer's life. God doesn't want His children to tough it out on their own; He wants them to turn to Him for the power and ability to live victoriously.

Evangelism and Missions

Question 44

Q. What should every follower of Jesus do for others?

A. Tell them about Jesus.

Matthew 28:18-20*; Mark 16:15; Luke 24:47; John 17:18

Note: Most Christians are familiar with the "Great Commission" at the end of Matthew, but actually each Gospel ends with a similar commission, and Acts begins with one. The emphasis is clear: all Christians should strive to tell other people about Jesus.

Question 45

Q. Why should believers tell others about Jesus?

A. It is our duty and our privilege.
  Matthew 28:18-20*; Romans 1:16; 10:14-15

Note: Although believers are commanded to tell others about Jesus, that should not be the only reason they do so. It is also important to realize that sharing Jesus with others is a joy and a privilege God gives. God could have designed angels to be evangelists, but He did not. He wants believers to experience impacting eternity instead.

Question 46

Q. What should our attitude be toward the lost?

A. Love and pity.
  Luke 10:25-37; John 3:16*; Romans 9:1-3

Note: Some Christians think that unbelievers are the enemy with which we are fighting. The Bible says that is not the case. Our enemy is Satan; lost people are men, women, and children who are trapped in his power and in need of God's forgiveness. We should therefore have compassion and pity for lost people.

Question 47

Q. How much of the world should we desire to see reached for Jesus?

A. All of the world.

Matthew 28:18-20*; John 3:16*; Acts 1:8

Note: While not many Christians would actually say it, many live as if God only cares about people of a certain race, nation, culture, economic class, or gender. The truth is that as Christians we should desire for the gospel to penetrate the entire world and for people of every people-group to come to saving faith in Jesus.

Question 48

Q. In what two ways do we try to win people to Jesus?

A. By telling them about Jesus and showing Jesus in how we live.

Matthew 9:35-38; 25:31-46; Romans 10:14-15

Note: The most effective way to be used by God to lead someone to saving faith in Jesus is by showing that person God's love at work in us and through us and by verbally explaining the gospel. If a person merely tries to explain the gospel without demonstrating its power, it will not be as effective. Conversely, no matter how much a person lives like Christ if he fails to explain the gospel message, others cannot be saved.

SUGGESTED MEMORY VERSES

January
"For God loved the world in this way: He gave His One and Only Son, so that everyone who believes in Him will not perish but have eternal life." **John 3:16**

February
"A thief comes only to steal and to kill and to destroy. I have come that they may have life and have it in abundance." **John 10:10**

March
Jesus told him, "I am the way, the truth, and the life. No one comes to the Father except through Me." **John 14:6**

April
For all have sinned and fall short of the glory of God. **Romans 3:23**

May
But God proves His own love for us in that while we were still sinners Christ died for us! **Romans 5:8**

June
For the wages of sin is death, but the gift of God is eternal life in Christ Jesus our Lord. **Romans 6:23**

July
For everyone who calls on the name of the Lord will be saved. **Romans 10:13**

August

For I passed on to you as most important what I also received: that Christ died for our sins according to the Scriptures, that He was buried, that He was raised on the third day according to the Scriptures. **1 Corinthians 15:3-4**

September

And He died for all so that those who live should no longer live for themselves, but for the One who died for them and was raised. **2 Corinthians 5:15**

October

Therefore if anyone is in Christ, there is a new creation; old things have passed away, and look, new things have come. **2 Corinthians 5:17**

November

For by grace you are saved through faith, and this is not from yourselves; it is God's gift—not from works, so that no one can boast. **Ephesians 2:8-9**

December

If we confess our sins, He is faithful and righteous to forgive us our sins and to cleanse us from all unrighteousness. **1 John 1:9**

UNIT 3

The Church

Question 1
Q. What is a church?
A. A local group of followers of Jesus.
Matthew 18:20; Acts 2:42; Ephesians 3:6

Note: The church is not a building or an activity. It is a group of people. However, it is not just any people. A church is delineated by being a group of followers of Jesus who are on mission for Christ and who meet regularly for worship, discipleship, evangelism, fellowship, and missions.

Question 2
Q. When did the church begin?
A. At Pentecost, 50 days after Jesus raised from the dead.
Matthew 16:18; Acts 2:1-4; 1 Corinthians 12:13

Note: Jesus spoke of the church in the future, so its start occurred after the Gospel narratives. The New Testament epistles speak to an existing church, so its start occurred before they were written. Based on the fact that Christians are given the Holy Spirit, the start of the church can be pinpointed to Pentecost in about A.D. 33 when the Holy Spirit was permanently given to those gathered in Jerusalem.

Question 3
Q. What unites a church?
A. The gospel of Jesus Christ.
Matthew 4:23; Mark 16:15; Galatians 1:6-10

Note: People are different with different opinions, desires, and priorities making it easy for a group of people to divide over issues. Just because that group of people happens to be comprised of Christians (in a church) doesn't mean it is easy to get along. For a church to thrive, it must keep the gospel of Jesus Christ central. If this happens, the expected differences between church members can be overcome and the people can be unified.

Question 4
Q. What is the gospel?
A. The good news of how people can be forgiven in Jesus.
1 Corinthians 15:1-8*

Note: The word "gospel" means "good news."

Question 5
Q. What is the purpose of the church?
A. To glorify God by taking the gospel to all of the world.
Matthew 28:18-20*; Acts 1:8; 1 Corinthians 10:31*

Note: The fundamental reason the church exists is to spread the gospel to the ends of the earth. While the church engages in a variety of activities, they all should occur under this overarching purpose. For example, it is important for churches to provide opportunities for members to grow in their relationship with Christ, however, the purpose of this is so they can better fulfill their mission to share Christ with others.

Question 6
Q. Who is head of the church?
A. Jesus.
Matthew 16:18; Colossians 1:18; Ephesians 1:22

Note: Jesus is the One who gives the church its vision and purpose. He is ultimately in control of the church and everyone is accountable to Him.

Question 7
Q. Who has Jesus appointed as leaders in the church?
A. Pastors, elders, and deacons.
Acts 6:1-6; 15:22; 1 Timothy 3:1-13

Note: There is disagreement concerning the identity of elders. Some believe that "elder" in the New Testament is another title for pastors, thus there would only be pastors and deacons. Others believe elders are a separate group and can be comprised of pastors and non-pastors. Regardless, Christ has given certain individuals in the local church delegated leadership authority under His overarching authority.

Question 8

Q. Who else makes decisions in a church?

A. Each member as they follow Jesus.
Acts 6:5; 15:22; 1 Peter 2:9

Note: While the local church has been given leaders who have some level of authority, the Bible also expresses the authority of the church body. At times we see the church leaders exerting authority in the Bible, at other times we see the church congregation making key decisions. The goal for the church should be for the leaders and church members to work together in harmony under the leadership of Jesus.

Question 9

Q. What is the universal church?

A. All believers, from all time, and everywhere.
Ephesians 1:22-23; 4:4; Philippians 2:2

Note: The local church (a local body of believers) is one part of the universal church (all believers). The phrases "visible" (local) and "invisible" (universal) church are sometimes used as well.

Question 10

Q. What two ordinances did Jesus give the church?

A. Baptism and the Lord's Supper.
Matthew 28:19; 1 Corinthians 11:24-26*

Note: An ordinance is a "religious ritual" or some activity in which the church engages regularly. Jesus gave two ordinances to the church when He commanded that believers be baptized and that His followers should participate in the Lord's Supper regularly until He returns.

Question 11

Q. Why did He give these two ordinances?

A. So we would remember that we belong to Jesus and what He did for us.

Matthew 28:19*; 1 Corinthians 11:24-26

Note: The purpose of both ordinances is for Christians to remember that we belong to Jesus (baptism) because we have accepted what He did for us on the cross (Lord's Supper).

Question 12

Q. What is baptism?

A. Immersing a believer underwater as a sign of being dead in sin and rising to new life.

Acts 2:41; Colossians 2:12; Romans 6:3-5

Note: The word "baptize" is taken straight from Greek and means to immerse. It is used outside of the Bible to describe a ship sinking.

Question 13

Q. Who should be baptized?

A. Only those who are true followers of Jesus as an act of obedience.

Matthew 3:6; Mark 16:16; Acts 18:8

Note: Because baptism pictures a person being dead in sin (when she is under the water) but then being raised to new life (when she is lifted up out of the water), it is only accurate for Christians. An unbeliever has not come up out of the water yet because he is still dead in sin (under the water).

Question 14

Q. What is the Lord's Supper?

A. Eating of the bread and drinking of the juice to remember the death and return of Jesus.

Mark 14:22-24; 1 Corinthians 10:16; 11:23-29

Note: Jesus instituted the Lord's Supper on the night of His betrayal and arrest. That night Jesus and the disciples were celebrating the Passover Meal (Exodus 12) which was a picture of God's deliverance of the children of Israel. Likewise, the Lord's Supper (or sometimes called "Communion") pictures God's deliverance of those who believe in Jesus because of the cross.

Question 15
Q. What does the bread represent?
A. The broken body of Jesus.
Matthew 26:26; 1 Corinthians 11:24

Note: The bread used at the original Lord's Supper would have been a flat bread with holes poked in it and stripes from how it was baked. These visuals add to the picture of Jesus' body being pierced on the cross and striped from the whippings He had received.

Question 16
Q. What does the juice represent?
A. The blood Jesus shed in His death.
Matthew 26:27-28; 1 Corinthians 11:25

Note: The Bible states that forgiveness of sin is not possible apart from the shedding of blood.

Question 17
Q. Who should participate in the Lord's Supper?
A. Only those who are true followers of Jesus.
1 Corinthians 10:16-7; 11:18, 20, 27-33

Note: Christians are expected to take participation in the Lord's Supper seriously and are instructed to examine their hearts for unconfessed sin and strained relationships. These should be handled before participating.

Question 18

Q. What is the Lord's Day?

A. Sunday, the first day of the week.

Luke 24:1-6; Acts 20:7; Revelation 1:10

Note: Some people confuse the Lord's Day and the Sabbath. The Sabbath is the last day of the week, Saturday, while the Lord's Day is the first day, Sunday.

Question 19

Q. What should we do on the Lord's Day?

A. Worship God with our church family.

Acts 20:7; 1 Corinthians 16:2; Colossians 3:16

Note: The early church began the practice of worshiping on the Lord's Day while evangelizing the Jews at the synagogue on the Sabbath.

Question 20

Q. Why do we worship on the Lord's Day?

A. It was the day when Jesus rose from the dead.

Luke 24:1-6; John 20:19,26; Acts 20:7

Note: God intended for Israel to observe the Sabbath (Exodus 31:12-18) so it is not wrong for the church to worship on Sunday instead. It is more fitting for the church to do so in light of Sunday being the day when Jesus rose from the dead.

Christian Living

Question 21
Q. From where do all blessings and good things come?
A. From God.
Matthew 7:11; Philippians 4:19*; James 1:17

Note: God is the source of all that is good. Nothing that is bad comes from God and at the same time nothing that is good comes from another source (such as the world or Satan). If you experience something good in your life then the credit should go to God.

Question 22
Q. Who owns all that we have?
A. God does. We are just stewards of the possessions He has given us.
Genesis 1:1*; Exodus 19:5; Psalm 50:10

Note: A common belief many Christians hold is that God requires us to give Him 10 percent of what we have, leaving the other 90 percent for us to use as we please. While we are instructed to give generously to the church as an investment in ministry (10 percent should be the standard), the rest is His as well.

Question 23

Q. What is a steward?

A. A person who takes care of someone else's possessions.
Matthew 25:14-30; Luke 12:42-48

Note: Christians are stewards of God's possessions which He has entrusted to us. As such, we are to use all of these possessions (finances, time, talents, etc) for God's glory. A good question to ask regularly is, "Am I using God's possession here for my good or for His good?"

Question 24

Q. What has God entrusted to us as His stewards?

A. Our time, talents, and possessions.
Romans 12:1; 1 Corinthians 41-2; 2 Timothy 2:2

Note: While most followers of Christ are aware of their need to invest their finances into ministry as good stewards, stewardship does not stop there. God has also given Christians time and talents which are to be used for His glory. And just as 10 percent of our finances is not the only amount we are to consider God's, we are to give God all of our time and talents.

Question 25
Q. Why should we serve God as His stewards?
A. To glorify God and help others.
Acts 2:44-47; 1 Corinthians 6:19-20; 10:31

Note: God's purpose in positioning Christians as His stewards is for them to experience joy, meaning, and purpose in their lives as they use what God has given them for His glory and to impact eternity.

Question 26
Q. How should we give our time, talents, and possessions to God?
A. Cheerfully, regularly, and generously.
1 Corinthians 16:1-4; 2 Corinthians 9:6-7

Note: The New Testament does not focus on a minimum standard we should give to God (again, because all that we have is God's). Instead, it prescribes that Christians give cheerfully and generously (according to their ability).

Question 27
Q. What is prayer?
A. Talking with God.
Genesis 17:22; Nehemiah 1:4-11; Philippians 4:6

Note: While the Bible offers outlines for praying, sample prayers, and various teachings on how to pray, we should not lose sight of the basic definition of prayer which is simply talking with God. It is better to define prayer as talking "with" God rather than talking "to" God because prayer should be a two-way conversation. While God will not speak audibly, we can hear from Him as He impresses His will upon our minds and hearts.

Question 28
Q. For what main thing should we pray?
A. For God's will to be done.
  Matthew 6:10; Luke 11:2

Note: God wants to know what we need and want when we pray. He also wants to know how we feel about things and for us to share our thoughts, concerns, and joys with Him. However, ultimately He wants us to seek His will for our lives when we talk with Him. We share all of the preceding things with God so that we may hear direction from Him.

Question 29
Q. What should be our goal of prayer?
A. To submit our will to God's.
  Luke 22:42; 2 Corinthians 12:8-10

Note: Many people pray with a goal of changing God; however, prayer should change us. Think of it this way, suppose a person who engages in unhealthy activities goes to his doctor for a check-up. The doctor tells him that he must stop these unhealthy behaviors or else he will die. What would you say to that person if he began to try to convince the doctor to change his advice? Who should be prepared to change, the doctor or the patient?

Question 30

Q. What should our attitude be as we submit to God's will?

A. With joy and without grumbling and complaining.
Philippians 2:14*; 1 Thessalonians 5:16

Note: It is often difficult for Christians to yield humbly to God's will. Often Christians know they should obey God but do so with pained expressions on their faces and bitterness in their hearts. Children tend to obey their parents the same way at times. Our goal should not be simple obedience; again that leads to legalism. Instead, our goal should be to love God to the degree that we obey Him with joy.

Question 31

Q. What is worship?

A. Declaring and celebrating the great worth of God.
Psalm 29:2; 95:6; John 4:23-24*

Note: Worship involves anything we do that declares and celebrates God, either as individuals or as part of a group. While music is most often associated with worship, it is far from the definition of it.

Question 32

Q. When should we worship God?

A. At all times, in all we do.
Romans 12:1; 1 Corinthians 10:31*

Note: We can enjoy God and recognize His beauty and worth in a variety of ways. Watching a sunset may prompt worship. Enjoying a meal with family and friends may lead to worship. Holding a child, sitting in silence, and enjoying a hobby can also all be part of worship. Be careful to understand though that these activities do not automatically lead to worship. We can enjoy a sunset without worshipping God if we fail to recognize that God is the Author of that sunset.

The Family

Question 33
Q. What is marriage?
A. The joining of one man and one woman in covenant relationship for a lifetime.
Genesis 2:15-25; Matthew 19:3-9; Mark 10:6-12

Note: While there is a difference of opinion concerning whether Christians may divorce and, if so, for what reasons, it is widely agreed that God's original design was for marriage to be permanent.

Question 34
Q. What does marriage picture?
A. The relationship between Jesus and the church.
Ephesians 5:22-33

Note: God wants Christians to have strong marriages for two important reasons. First, having strong marriages is the best way to have strong families. Strong families, in turn, is the best way to pass on the gospel from generation to generation and to experience healthy societies. As important as that is, God has a greater purpose for Christians to have strong marriages. Marriage is used throughout the Bible as a picture of the church's relationship with Christ. If the church is comprised of couples with weak, flawed marriages, that hinders the important picture of our relationship with Christ.

Question 35
Q. Who is superior in marriage?
A. No one. The husband and wife are of equal worth before God.
1 Corinthians 12:13; Galatians 3:28; Colossians 3:11

Note: While the husband and wife are equals before God, that does not mean that they do not have different roles and perform different functions within marriage. The same is true of the church. While all believers are of equal value to God, they still have different roles and functions within the church.

Question 36
Q. What is the husband's main role in marriage?
A. To love his wife as Jesus loves the church.
Ephesians 5:25-33; Colossians 3:19; 1 Peter 3:7

Note: While controversial, the Bible positions the husband as head (leader) of the marriage. This leadership role is often misunderstood and abused and some husbands have used it in defense of sinful behavior. That is not God's plan. His plan is for husbands to lead their wives as servant-leaders who love their wives to the degree that Christ loves the church. Christ's love for the church prompted Him to selflessly sacrifice Himself for it. Husbands should seek to do the same for their wives.

Question 37
Q. What else should the husband do?
A. He should provide for his family, protect them, and lead them.
Psalm 128; Ephesians 6:4; 1 Timothy 5:8

Note: The father has been given the important role of physically, emotionally, and spiritually providing for His family. While ultimately all of those provisions come from God, the father is supposed to seek God's will as a servant for his family.

Question 38
Q. What is the wife's main role in marriage?
A. To submit to her husband, the servant-leader of the home.
Ephesians 5:22-24,33; Colossians 3:18; 1 Peter 3:1-6

Note: Wives submit by willingly and joyfully placing themselves under the God-given, loving, and sacrificial leadership of their husbands. This does not suggest wives are of lesser value, nor does it infer that wives should be "door mats" allowing sinful husbands to walk over them. When God's plan is followed by the believing husband and wife, the marriage and home is strongest and most joyful.

Question 39

Q. What are all children?

A. A blessing from God.
  Psalm 127:3-5; James 1:17

Note: All children are gifts and blessings from God. While being a parent is at times difficult and trying, this fundamental truth should saturate a parent's perspective, communication, and interaction with his or her child.

Question 40

Q. What are parents to teach their children?

A. The gospel.
  Deuteronomy 6:4-9*; Psalm 78:1-8; 127:1-5

Note: Parents, and fathers more specifically, have been given this role by God. The church exists, in part, to help parents fulfill this ministry, not to replace them. A biblical church should help parents learn to communicate the gospel to their children and should reinforce what the parents are teaching at home.

Question 41

Q. What should children do?

A. Honor and obey their parents.
  Exodus 20:12; Ephesians 6:1-3; Colossians 3:20*

Note: Just as we are to obey God with love, children are commanded to honor (love and respect) their parents as they obey them.

Last Things

Question 42
Q. Where is Jesus now?
A. At the right hand of God the Father.
Colossians 3:1; Hebrews 1:3; 12:2

Note: The Bible tells us that when Jesus came to earth, He left His position at the Father's side in heaven and that when He ascended He returned to that place. The right hand position is a place of honor and authority.

Question 43
Q. Will Jesus return to earth again?
A. Yes, He will come again for His church and to judge the world.
Matthew 25:31-42; 2 Thessalonians 1:7-10; Revelation 19

Note: A fundamental promise that gives Christians everywhere hope is that Jesus is returning one day for His followers. This is good news for people who have accepted God's gift of salvation, but not good news for those who refuse Christ. Christ's first appearance on earth was as the Suffering Servant; His return will be as the Conquering King.

Question 44
Q. When will Jesus return?

A. In God's perfect timing that is unknown to us.
Acts 1:7; Romans 8:23, 25; Philippians 3:20

Note: Christ's return is unknown, but we do know that it can occur at anytime. This is why we are instructed to spend our time and resources wisely as good stewards so that we are not caught "asleep" when Jesus returns.

Question 45
Q. What will happen to the dead when Jesus returns?

A. They will be raised.
Daniel 12:2; John 5:28-29; Acts 24:14-15

Note: Both dead believers and dead unbelievers will be raised from the dead. The Bible teaches that everyone has eternal life; it just depends on whether that eternal life will be with Christ or apart from Him.

Question 46
Q. What will happens to believer when Jesus returns?

A. They live with God forever in a new heaven and new earth.
1 Thessalonians 4:16-17; 2 Peter 3:10-3; Revelation 21:1-4

Note: When Christ returns for His church, believers will enjoy unhindered fellowship with Christ as was originally intended. Many Christians struggle to be excited about spending eternity with Christ because they wrongly believe it will simply be one long, boring worship service. This is far from true. While believers will worship Christ in a formal, corporate setting, we will also engage in several other activities such as working for God, enjoying fellowship with one another, and worshipping God through various activities as we do now.

Question 47

Q. What will happen to people who do not believe in Jesus at judgment?

A. They will be cast into the lake of fire.
Matthew 25:41, 46; 2 Thessalonians 1:8-9; Revelation 20:12-15

Note: All unbelievers, Satan, and the demons will be cast into the lake of fire where they will spend eternity fully conscious of their surroundings.

Question 48

Q. What is the lake of fire?

A. It is a place of total separation from having a relationship with God with nothing good.
Matthew 25:46; Mark 9:43-8; Luke 16:19-31

Note: The lake of fire will lack anything good because God is the source of all good. Unbelievers will experience the pain, isolation, and penalty of their rebellion against God and rejection of Jesus for eternity. Knowing this should lead Christians to extend love and compassion toward lost people and to fuel evangelism and missions efforts.

SUGGESTED MEMORY VERSES

January

"Haven't I commanded you: be strong and courageous? Do not be afraid or discouraged, for the LORD your God is with you wherever you go." **Joshua 1:9**

February

The LORD is my shepherd; there is nothing I lack. He lets me lie down in green pastures; He leads me beside quiet waters. He renews my life; He leads me along the right paths for His name's sake. Even when I go through the darkest valley, I fear no danger, for You are with me; Your rod and Your staff—they comfort me. You prepare a table before me in the presence of my enemies; You anoint my head with oil; my cup overflows. Only goodness and faithful love will pursue me all the days of my life, and I will dwell in the house of the LORD as long as I live. **Psalm 23:1-6**

March

Trust in the LORD with all your heart, and do not rely on your own understanding; think about Him in all your ways, and He will guide you on the right paths. **Proverbs 3:5-6**

April

The father of a righteous son will rejoice greatly, and one who fathers a wise son will delight in him. Let your father and mother have joy, and let her who gave birth to you rejoice. **Proverbs 23:24-25**

May

Be alert, stand firm in the faith, be brave and strong. Your every action must be done with love. **1 Corinthians 16:13-14**

June

I have been crucified with Christ; and I no longer live, but Christ lives in me. The life I now live in the flesh, I live by faith in the Son of God, who loved me and gave Himself for me. **Galatians 2:20**

July

And be kind and compassionate to one another, forgiving one another, just as God also forgave you in Christ. **Ephesians 4:32**

August

Do everything without grumbling and arguing. **Philippians 2:14**

September

And my God will supply all your needs according to His riches in glory in Christ Jesus. **Philippians 4:19**

October

And whatever you do, in word or in deed, do everything in the name of the Lord Jesus, giving thanks to God the Father through Him. **Colossians 3:17**

November

Children, obey your parents in everything, for this is pleasing in the Lord. **Colossians 3:20**

December

Now if any of you lacks wisdom, he should ask God, who gives to all generously and without criticizing, and it will be given to him. **James 1:5**

ABOUT THE AUTHOR

Dr. Brian Dembowczyk has been a pastor for over 15 years at churches in Florida, Maryland, and Kentucky. He has served in a variety of roles including senior pastor, discipleship pastor, executive pastor, and student & family pastor. Brian earned an M.Div. from the Southern Baptist Theological Seminary (Louisville, Kentucky) and a D.Min. from the New Orleans Baptist Theological Seminary (New Orleans, Louisiana), where he serves as an extension campus adjunct professor. He also is a frequent contributor to several LifeWay Christian Resources publications including *ParentLife* magazine. Brian and his wife, Tara, have three children: Joshua, Hannah, and Caleb.

59695554R00048

Made in the USA
Lexington, KY
12 January 2017